A Comprehensive English Language Test for Learners of English

Form A
Test Book:
Includes Listening,
Structure, and
Vocabulary Sections

by David P. Harris and Leslie A. Palmer

Boston, Massachusetts   Burr Ridge, Illinois
Dubuque, Iowa   Madison, Wisconsin   New York, New York
San Francisco, California   St. Louis, Missouri

DO NOT OPEN THIS TEST BOOK UNTIL YOU ARE TOLD TO DO SO

ISBN 0·07·026871·1 Comprehensive English Language Test: Form A

14 15 16 17 18 19 BKM BKM 9 0 9 8 7 6 5 4 3 2 1 0

Printed in the United States of America.

CELT ▷

Form A

General Directions

1. This is a test of your ability to use the English language. It is in three sections, and there are special directions for each section.

2. Each section of the test has a time limit, and you will be told when to go on to the next section. If you complete a section before time is called, you may go back and check your answers.

3. Try to answer every problem. If you are not sure of the correct answer, make the best guess that you can. Your score on the test will be based on the number of correct answers that you give.

4. Do not put any marks in this test book. You must put *all* your answers on the separate answer sheet you have been given. To mark an answer, find the number of the problem on the answer sheet and put an x in the space over the letter A, B, C, or D — whichever goes with the answer you have chosen.

5. Mark only *one answer* for each problem. If you change your mind about an answer after you have marked it on the answer sheet, completely erase your first answer and then mark your new answer.

6. Be sure that you have printed your name and the other information that is asked for at the top of the answer sheet.

DO NOT TURN THE PAGE UNTIL YOU ARE TOLD TO DO SO

Section One
LISTENING

Part I: Answering Questions

Directions: In this part of the test you will hear 20 questions. Each question will be spoken *just one time,* and it will *not* be written out for you. Therefore, you must listen very carefully. After you hear a question, read the four possible answers that are printed in this test book and decide which one would make the *best answer* to the question you have heard. Then find the number of the problem on your answer sheet and mark your answer by putting an × in the space over the letter A, B, C, or D — whichever goes with the answer you have chosen.

Listen to the following example.

> **You will hear:** "When are you going to New York?"
>
> **You will read:** (A) To visit my brother.
> (B) By plane.
> (C) Next Friday.
> (D) Yes, I am.

The best answer to the question "When are you going to New York?" is choice (C), *Next Friday.* Therefore, if this problem were in the test, you would find the number of the problem on your answer sheet and mark choice (C) as shown below.

$$( ) \quad ( ) \quad (\times) \quad ( )$$
$$A \quad\quad B \quad\quad C \quad\quad D$$

This is the way to mark all the problems in Part I.

Now let us begin the test with question number 1.

1. (A) Yes, I do.
   (B) About twenty minutes.
   (C) Take a Number 30.
   (D) Yes, you should.

2. (A) Yes, I will.
   (B) Just $50.
   (C) Yes, I have to.
   (D) Just two days.

3. (A) I believe he does.
   (B) I think it's a drugstore.
   (C) Yes, it's his own.
   (D) Yes, he's very kind.

4. (A) Since last April.
   (B) Yes, I do.
   (C) At the new Hilton Hotel.
   (D) Until the end of this month.

Go on to the next page.

5. (A) About noon.
   (B) By bus.
   (C) To the baseball game.
   (D) Certainly we should.

6. (A) Until about ten o'clock.
   (B) Yes, I usually do.
   (C) At my brother's house.
   (D) Yes, in the evening.

7. (A) Yes, I see her.
   (B) They're very nice.
   (C) Yes, I see them.
   (D) Whenever they come to Washington.

8. (A) Yes, I often used to.
   (B) It was Mary's.
   (C) Yes, I took them.
   (D) I'm quite used to it now.

9. (A) Yes, I always do.
   (B) In the library.
   (C) Right after dinner.
   (D) Yes, I did.

10. (A) At the new department store.
    (B) No more than $40.
    (C) As soon as you can.
    (D) Yes, I think you should.

11. (A) I'll be glad to.
    (B) Yes, he did.
    (C) At about four o'clock.
    (D) No, he hasn't.

12. (A) Yes, I do.
    (B) Next fall, I believe.
    (C) Yes, she does.
    (D) It's an excellent idea.

13. (A) It's hanging in the hall.
    (B) Yes, it's tonight.
    (C) At about eight o'clock.
    (D) Yes, I think you should.

14. (A) Yes, he does.
    (B) In two days.
    (C) Since 1984.
    (D) By plane.

15. (A) Yes, it will be the last one.
    (B) At eight o'clock.
    (C) No more than two hours.
    (D) Yes, it begins in an hour.

16. (A) I've just met him once.
    (B) Yes, he's quite well now.
    (C) I've known her for years.
    (D) Yes, I certainly do.

17. (A) Yes, on the hall table.
    (B) No, I don't know when he left.
    (C) No, I don't know where he is.
    (D) Yes, I know he did.

18. (A) Yes, Mary has two sisters.
    (B) No, one is a teacher.
    (C) Yes, Mary has two nurses.
    (D) No, Mary is a doctor.

19. (A) No, he isn't here just now.
    (B) About once a month.
    (C) Very little, really.
    (D) Yes, I can hear him.

20. (A) Yes, she likes him very much.
    (B) He's a very amusing man.
    (C) Yes, George likes her very much.
    (D) She's a very charming woman.

This is the end of Part I. Now turn the page and listen to the directions to Part II as they are read to you.

Part II: Understanding Statements

Directions: In this part of the test you will hear 20 statements. Each statement will be spoken *just one time,* and it will *not* be written out for you. After you hear a statement, read the four sentences that are printed in this test book and decide which one is *closest in meaning* to the statement you have heard. Then find the number of the problem on your answer sheet and mark your answer by putting an × in the space over the letter A, B, C, or D — whichever goes with the sentence you have chosen.

Listen to the following example.

You will hear: "George has just returned home from his vacation."

You will read: (A) George is spending his vacation at home.
(B) George has just finished his vacation.
(C) George is just about to begin his vacation.
(D) George has decided not to take a vacation.

Choice (B), *George has just finished his vacation,* is closest in meaning to the statement you heard, "George has just returned home from his vacation." Therefore, choice (B) is the answer to this problem and you would mark your answer sheet as shown below.

( )   (×)   ( )   ( )
A   B   C   D

This is the way to mark all the problems in Part II.

Now let us begin Part II with problem number 21.

21. (A) Jim likes neither tea nor coffee.
(B) Jim likes tea better than coffee.
(C) Jim likes coffee just as much as tea.
(D) Jim likes coffee better than tea.

22. (A) Paul came to visit us.
(B) Paul sent us a letter.
(C) Paul attempted to call us.
(D) Paul wanted to help us.

23. (A) We had trouble finding Carl's letter.
(B) Carl had trouble reading the letter.
(C) We had trouble reading Carl's letter.
(D) Carl had trouble finding the letter.

24. (A) I think George is a poor driver.
(B) I've never seen George drive.
(C) I think Helen is a poor driver.
(D) I've never seen Helen drive.

25. (A) We couldn't find John's homework.
(B) The homework was difficult for John.
(C) We couldn't understand John's homework.
(D) John thought the homework was easy.

26. (A) Mary has found the children.
(B) Mary raised the children herself.
(C) Mary likes the children very much.
(D) Mary is playing with the children.

27. (A) We saw Harry although he was late.
(B) We saw Harry although we were late.
(C) We didn't see Harry because he was late.
(D) We were too late to see Harry.

Go on to the next page.

28. (A) Bob will be here but Betty won't.
    (B) Neither Bob nor Betty can come.
    (C) Betty will be here but Bob won't.
    (D) Both Betty and Bob can come.

29. (A) There were 50 people in the theater.
    (B) There were 75 people in the theater.
    (C) There were 100 people in the theater.
    (D) There were 150 people in the theater.

30. (A) We were sorry that Ruth didn't attend the party.
    (B) Neither Ruth nor we attended the party.
    (C) We enjoyed attending the party with Ruth.
    (D) Ruth enjoyed the party more than we did.

31. (A) The Smiths left at eleven-thirty.
    (B) The Smiths left at twelve o'clock.
    (C) The Smiths left at twelve-thirty.
    (D) The Smiths left at one o'clock.

32. (A) Alice wants the box.
    (B) Alice wants the suit.
    (C) Alice wants the hat.
    (D) Alice wants the case.

33. (A) There probably are six eggs left.
    (B) There probably are eight eggs left.
    (C) There probably are ten eggs left.
    (D) There probably are sixteen eggs left.

34. (A) Mary didn't believe what John said.
    (B) Mary believed what I told John.
    (C) Mary didn't believe what I told John.
    (D) Mary believed what John said.

35. (A) We took the train and it was late.
    (B) We took the bus and it was on time.
    (C) We took the train and it was on time.
    (D) We took the bus and it was late.

36. (A) We had just seen a movie when we met Helen.
    (B) Helen was going to a movie when we met her.
    (C) Helen had just seen a movie when we met her.
    (D) We were going to a movie when we met Helen.

37. (A) Jane and Ann are very different.
    (B) Jane doesn't like her sister.
    (C) Jane and her sister are alike.
    (D) Jane doesn't like Ann's sister.

38. (A) Only Jack's first attempt was successful.
    (B) Only Jack's second attempt was successful.
    (C) Both of Jack's attempts were successful.
    (D) Neither of Jack's attempts was successful.

39. (A) Paul likes living here very much now.
    (B) Paul hasn't become accustomed to our climate yet.
    (C) Paul used to like living here, but he doesn't anymore.
    (D) Paul is accustomed to our climate now.

40. (A) We haven't known her long, and neither has Bill.
    (B) We've known her longer than Bill has.
    (C) Bill has known her longer than he's known us.
    (D) Bill has known her longer than we have.

This is the end of Part II. Now turn the page and listen to the directions to Part III as they are read to you.

Part III: Comprehending Dialogues

Directions: In this part of the test you will hear 10 short conversations between a man and a woman. You will hear each conversation *just one time,* and it will *not* be written out for you. At the end of each conversation, a third voice will ask a question about what was said. After you hear a conversation and the question about it, read the four possible answers that are printed in this test book and decide which one is the *best answer* to the question you were asked. Then find the number of the problem on your answer sheet and put an × in the space over the letter A, B, C, or D — whichever goes with the answer you have chosen.

Listen to the following example.

You will hear:	(man)	"Are you still planning to leave for New York next Monday?"
	(woman)	"I'm afraid not. My husband just found out he'll be in a meeting until late that afternoon, so we won't be able to get started until the following morning."
	(3rd voice)	On what day does the woman expect to leave for New York?
You will read:	(A) Sunday	
	(B) Monday	
	(C) Tuesday	
	(D) Wednesday	

From the conversation we learn that the woman and her husband cannot leave on Monday, but will have to wait until the following morning, which would be Tuesday. Therefore, the correct answer to the question is choice (C), which you would mark on your answer sheet after the number of the problem.

$$(\ ) \quad (\ ) \quad (\times) \quad (\ )$$
$$A \quad B \quad C \quad D$$

Now let us begin Part III with problem number 41.

Go on to the next page.

41. (A) He liked it, but she didn't.
    (B) She liked it, but he didn't.
    (C) Both of them liked it.
    (D) Neither of them liked it.

42. (A) That Helen is still in the hospital.
    (B) That Helen's friend is still in the hospital.
    (C) That Helen's brother is still in the hospital.
    (D) That Helen's boy is still in the hospital.

43. (A) Take the children to the beach.
    (B) Get her coat at the cleaner's.
    (C) Take her and the children to dinner.
    (D) Get something at the post office.

44. (A) Fifty cents.
    (B) Seventy-five cents.
    (C) Eighty cents.
    (D) One dollar.

45. (A) She visited George's parents in Chicago.
    (B) She visited her sister in Boston.
    (C) She visited George's parents in Boston.
    (D) She visited her sister in Chicago.

46. (A) In a doctor's office.
    (B) In a clothing store.
    (C) In a shoe repair shop.
    (D) In a furniture store.

47. (A) That he has decided to look for a house.
    (B) That he is moving to a new apartment.
    (C) That he has bought a house.
    (D) That he has decided to stay where he is.

48. (A) Thirty cents.
    (B) Forty cents.
    (C) Fifty cents.
    (D) Sixty cents.

49. (A) In a bus station.
    (B) In a ticket office.
    (C) In a bank.
    (D) In a furniture store.

50. (A) Six-thirty (6:30).
    (B) Seven o'clock (7:00).
    (C) Seven-thirty (7:30).
    (D) Eight o'clock (8:00).

*This is the end of the Listening Section.
Do not turn the page until you are told to
do so.*

CELT

Form A

LISTENING
STRUCTURE
VOCABULARY

General Directions

1. This is a test of your ability to use the English language. It is in three sections, and there are special directions for each section.

2. Each section of the test has a time limit, and you will be told when to go on to the next section. If you complete a section before time is called, you may go back and check your answers.

3. Try to answer every problem. If you are not sure of the correct answer, make the best guess that you can. Your score on the test will be based on the number of correct answers that you give.

4. Do not put any marks in this test book. You must put *all* your answers on the separate answer sheet you have been given. To mark an answer, find the number of the problem on the answer sheet and put an x in the space over the letter A, B, C, or D— whichever goes with the answer you have chosen.

5. Mark only *one answer* for each problem. If you change your mind about an answer after you have marked it on the answer sheet, completely erase your first answer and then mark your new answer.

6. Be sure that you have printed your name and the other information that is asked for at the top of the answer sheet.

DO NOT TURN THE PAGE UNTIL YOU ARE TOLD TO DO SO

Section Two
STRUCTURE

Directions: This section of the test is designed to measure how well you know the grammar of English. There are 75 problems, and you will be given 45 minutes to do them. Each problem represents a brief conversation between two persons. In each of the conversations, one or more words have been omitted. Four words or phrases, marked (A), (B), (C), and (D), appear beneath each problem. You are to choose the *one* word or phrase that a native English speaker would use to complete the conversation.

Look at Example I.

Example I: "How old is George?"

"He's two years younger _____ his brother Paul."

(A) that
(B) of
(C) as
(D) than

In English, we would say: "He's two years younger *than* his brother Paul." Therefore, if this problem were in the test, you would find the number of the problem on your answer sheet and mark choice (D) as shown below.

Example I: ( ) ( ) ( ) (×)
         A   B   C   D

Now look at Example II.

Example II: "Have you finished the report for Mr. Jones?"

"Yes, I _____ this morning."

(A) it to him gave
(B) gave it to him
(C) to him gave it
(D) gave to him it

The native speaker would choose choice (B), "Yes, I *gave it to him* this morning," as the best way to complete this conversation. If this problem were in the test, you would mark choice (B) on your answer sheet as shown below.

Example II: ( ) (×) ( ) ( )
         A   B   C   D

Now turn the page and begin work on the test problems.

1. "Did you have lunch with your brother yesterday?"

   "No. I waited _____ two hours, but he never came."

   (A) by
   (B) since
   (C) for
   (D) until

2. "Is this Sue's coat?"

   "Yes, I think it's _____ ."

   (A) hers
   (B) of her
   (C) her
   (D) of hers

3. "Did you enjoy visiting the Empire State Building?"

   "Yes, I believe it's _____ building in the world."

   (A) tallest
   (B) the most tall
   (C) the taller
   (D) the tallest

4. "Someone left this book in the classroom."

   "See if _____ a name inside it."

   (A) is there
   (B) it may be
   (C) there is
   (D) it is

5. "I hear the Smiths bought a new house."

   "Yes. They bought the one _____ ."

   (A) next to our
   (B) next to ours
   (C) next of ours
   (D) next from our

6. "Where's Bob?"

   "I just saw him in the _____ ."

   (A) lunches room
   (B) room of lunches
   (C) room for lunches
   (D) lunch room

7. "May I please see Mr. Wilson?"

   "I'm sorry, but he _____ ."

   (A) any more doesn't live here
   (B) doesn't any more live here
   (C) doesn't live any more here
   (D) doesn't live here any more

8. "Did Lisa pass the test too?"

   "Yes. In fact her score was the same _____ ."

   (A) to mine
   (B) with me
   (C) as mine
   (D) to me

9. "I saw the Johnsons at the bank today."

   "They've been on vacation, _____ ?"

   (A) aren't they
   (B) haven't they
   (C) weren't they
   (D) hadn't they

10. "Let's get a cup of coffee."

    "Not now. I don't want to stop _____ yet."

    (A) study
    (B) to study
    (C) for studying
    (D) studying

11. "Can you read the sign on the door now?"

    "No. Please hold _____ ."

    (A) the light a little closer to it
    (B) the light to it a little closer
    (C) a little closer the light to it
    (D) to it the light a little closer

Go on to the next page.

12. "Why isn't the painting done yet?"

    "John _____ his share of the work yesterday."

    (A) doesn't
    (B) didn't do
    (C) doesn't do
    (D) didn't

13. "Have you seen Frank recently?"

    "No, I guess he must _____ away on vacation."

    (A) be
    (B) being
    (C) been
    (D) to be

14. "We've finally decided we ought to try to sell our old car."

    "How long _____ it?"

    (A) you've had
    (B) have you
    (C) had you
    (D) have you had

15. "I don't see Betty anywhere."

    "She'll be right back. She just went out _____ Bill."

    (A) to calling
    (B) for call
    (C) to call
    (D) for calling

16. "How did you like the lectures?"

    "I thought they were _____ ."

    (A) interested
    (B) interest
    (C) interesting
    (D) of interests

17. "Did you hear that Bill finally sold his house?"

    "Yes, but I don't know who _____ it."

    (A) bought
    (B) buys
    (C) had bought
    (D) did buy

18. "The old Smith house is certainly in bad condition."

    "There's nobody living there now, _____ ?"

    (A) is it
    (B) is there
    (C) do they
    (D) is he

19. "Do you know how to work this radio?"

    "Yes. It's very similar _____ mine."

    (A) of
    (B) to
    (C) from
    (D) with

20. "Do you want to go to the bank with me?"

    "No, thank you. I think I'll wait until the mail _____ ."

    (A) should come
    (B) is coming
    (C) comes
    (D) will come

Go on to the next page.

21. "We can eat dinner either before or after the show."

    "Which _____ do?"

    (A) would you rather
    (B) do you rather
    (C) you would rather
    (D) will you rather

22. "That's a beautiful coat in the window."

    "It certainly is. If I had the money, _____ buy it."

    (A) I'll
    (B) I may
    (C) I shall
    (D) I'd

23. "Won't Mark come with us?"

    "No, he said he wasn't interested _____ swimming."

    (A) in going
    (B) for going
    (C) going
    (D) to going

24. "I see the Director coming down the hall."

    "Then we'd better quit _____ and get back to work."

    (A) talk
    (B) from talking
    (C) talking
    (D) to talk

25. "There's a very good program on television at eight tonight."

    "Maybe we'll get home _____ to see it."

    (A) enough early
    (B) so early
    (C) early enough
    (D) so early enough

26. "We'll be ready to leave at six."

    "Well, Mike certainly _____ to be back by then."

    (A) must
    (B) ought
    (C) can
    (D) should

27. "Are you going downtown?"

    "Yes. _____ to do some shopping."

    (A) I'd like
    (B) I'll like
    (C) I like
    (D) I'm liking

28. "Have you moved into your new house?"

    "No. It _____ until next month."

    (A) won't finish
    (B) isn't finishing
    (C) doesn't finish
    (D) won't be finished

29. "No one was prepared for Dr. Grey's questions."

    "We _____ have read the lesson last night."

    (A) should
    (B) can
    (C) would
    (D) ought

30. "The children are coming back from their walk."

    "Don't let them come in without _____ their wet shoes."

    (A) they've taken off
    (B) to take off
    (C) taking off
    (D) they'll take off

31. "May I help you?"

    "Yes, please. I would like to look at _____ ."

    (A) table lamps
    (B) tables lamp
    (C) table lamp
    (D) tables lamps

Go on to the next page.

32. "Haven't you been outside all afternoon?"

"No. How much snow _____ on the ground now?"

(A) it is
(B) is it
(C) there is
(D) is there

33. "This lamp looks terrible since the baby knocked it over."

"I agree. Why don't you get rid _____ ?"

(A) of it
(B) from it
(C) it
(D) with it

34. "What did the policeman say to you?"

"He told us _____ so noisy."

(A) don't to be
(B) not to be
(C) we shouldn't been
(D) not to been

35. "Do the students in your class study a lot?"

"Some of them do. _____ just don't care."

(A) Anothers
(B) The other
(C) Some other
(D) Others

36. "I wish we'd gone to the beach this weekend."

"You should _____ it sooner."

(A) mentioned
(B) had mentioned
(C) to mention
(D) have mentioned

37. "When do you think we'll leave tomorrow?"

"You'd better _____ ready at eight o'clock."

(A) to be
(B) be
(C) being
(D) been

38. "Isn't old Mr. Brown coming to the meeting tonight?"

"I doubt it; _____ ."

(A) he hardly ever leaves his house now
(B) hardly ever he leaves his house now
(C) he hardly leaves his house ever now
(D) he leaves hardly ever his house now

39. "Would you like to go to a movie tonight?"

"No, thanks. I'm _____ tired to go anywhere."

(A) so
(B) much
(C) too
(D) quite

40. "Was the job difficult?"

"Yes, we found _____ ."

(A) the work hard for doing
(B) hard to do the work
(C) it hard for doing the work
(D) the work hard to do

41. "Will you go home this weekend?"

"No, and _____ ."

(A) neither George will
(B) George won't too
(C) neither will George
(D) so won't George

42. "Here are the books you wanted."

"Would you mind _____ on the desk, please?"

(A) to put them
(B) putting them
(C) put them
(D) to them putting

Go on to the next page.

43. "Did you meet Nancy White at the party?"

    "No, _____ by the time I arrived."

    (A) she was left
    (B) she's left
    (C) she'd left
    (D) she must leave

44. "You've come just in time to help us, Tom."

    "Fine. What needs _____ ?"

    (A) to do
    (B) done
    (C) to be done
    (D) I do

45. "Were any of the Smiths hurt in the fire?"

    "No, and the firemen got _____ to save their house."

    (A) quickly enough there
    (B) there quickly enough
    (C) there enough quickly
    (D) enough quickly there

46. "Isn't your radio very much like your brother's?"

    "Yes, they're exactly _____ ."

    (A) sames
    (B) likes
    (C) same
    (D) alike

47. "What did the boys buy?"

    "Nothing but a couple of _____ ."

    (A) thirty-cents candies bars
    (B) thirty-cent candy bars
    (C) thirty-cent candies bars
    (D) thirty-cents candy bars

48. "I'd like some more coffee, please."

    "I'm sorry, but there doesn't seem to be _____ ."

    (A) any left
    (B) left any
    (C) leaving any
    (D) some left

49. "Paul's been ill for several days now."

    "I know; I wish _____ see a doctor."

    (A) he should
    (B) he can
    (C) he'll
    (D) he'd

50. "Mary has had a lot of teaching experience, hasn't she?"

    "Yes, indeed. _____ English since 1970."

    (A) She's taught
    (B) She's teaching
    (C) She was teaching
    (D) She'd taught

51. "Have you heard from Bill recently?"

    "Yes. I got a letter yesterday, but there wasn't _____ news in it."

    (A) some
    (B) much
    (C) many
    (D) lots

52. "Do you still have your job at the bank?"

    "Oh, no. _____ there for the past two years."

    (A) I don't work
    (B) I haven't worked
    (C) I'm not working
    (D) I didn't work

Go on to the next page.

53. "We're all going to the movie tonight."

"I wish _____ go with you, but I have to finish my homework."

(A) I can
(B) I'll
(C) I could
(D) I'd

54. "What does Mrs. Williams do for a living?"

"She owns one of the best _____ in the city."

(A) dress shop
(B) dresses shops
(C) dresses shop
(D) dress shops

55. "Can you carry all those boxes?"

"Yes. They're _____ than they look."

(A) more lighter
(B) much lighter
(C) more light
(D) very lighter

56. "Have you ever studied French?"

"No, but I wish I _____ ."

(A) have
(B) do
(C) had
(D) will

57. "Isn't it getting dark early tonight?"

"I think so; I see _____ is on already."

(A) the street light
(B) the light of the street
(C) the street's light
(D) the light street

58. "Did you have trouble with your car this morning?"

"Yes, but I finally managed _____ ."

(A) to get starting it
(B) it to get started
(C) to get it started
(D) getting started it

59. "Is Martha very sick?"

"No, _____ a little cold."

(A) she's just got
(B) she just gets
(C) she's just get
(D) she just gots

60. "Where did you see the notice of the meeting?"

"It was on _____ of tonight's paper."

(A) page second
(B) the page two
(C) the page second
(D) page two

61. "I'd met Mr. Jones many times before last night."

"So _____ ."

(A) did I
(B) had I
(C) I had
(D) I did

Go on to the next page.

62. "Are Carla and Jane still here?"

    "Yes, the storm prevented them _____ yesterday."

    (A) leave
    (B) to leave
    (C) from leaving
    (D) of leaving

63. "Did you hear the six o'clock news?"

    "No, I forgot to listen _____ ."

    (A) it
    (B) them
    (C) to them
    (D) to it

64. "I'm sorry to have to leave, but I've got to catch my train."

    "I've enjoyed _____ to talk with you."

    (A) to be able
    (B) being able
    (C) to been able
    (D) of being able

65. "Were you able to borrow Helen's camera?"

    "No, she said _____ lend it to anyone."

    (A) she'll rather not
    (B) she wouldn't rather
    (C) she'd rather not
    (D) she doesn't rather

66. "Do you still plan to go to Miami this vacation?"

    "Yes, and I wish you'd consider _____ with us."

    (A) going
    (B) that you'll go
    (C) to go
    (D) to going

67. "Did Harry see Professor Carr yesterday?"

    "He did, and the Professor gave him one of the best _____ I've ever heard."

    (A) piece of advice
    (B) pieces of advices
    (C) piece of advices
    (D) pieces of advice

68. "Will the Smiths be going abroad this summer?"

    "No, they finally decided _____ ."

    (A) not going
    (B) not to
    (C) not to be
    (D) not to going

69. "Let's stay in New York another day."

    "Fine, but we _____ better change our plane reservations then."

    (A) have
    (B) would
    (C) will
    (D) had

Go on to the next page.

70. "We just saw John at the bookstore."

"That's strange; I didn't think he _____ back until tomorrow."

(A) will come
(B) was to come
(C) is coming
(D) is to come

71. "I wish Bill would drive us to the train station."

"He has _____ to take us all."

(A) too small a car
(B) very small a car
(C) a too small car
(D) such small a car

72. "Will you and your brother visit your parents this summer?"

"I imagine _____ ."

(A) it
(B) that
(C) so
(D) we'll

73. "Haven't you eaten yet?"

"No, and I'm not used _____ so long without lunch."

(A) to go
(B) to going
(C) that I go
(D) of going

74. "How was your examination?"

"It wasn't very difficult, but it was _____ long."

(A) too much
(B) so much
(C) very much
(D) much too

75. "Have you heard that Peter is going home tomorrow?"

"No, I thought he _____ until next week."

(A) wasn't going
(B) won't go
(C) isn't going
(D) doesn't go

This is the end of the Structure Section. Do not turn the page until you are told to do so.

CELT →

Form A
LISTENING
STRUCTURE
VOCABULARY

General Directions

1. This is a test of your ability to use the English language. It is in three sections, and there are special directions for each section.

2. Each section of the test has a time limit, and you will be told when to go on to the next section. If you complete a section before time is called, you may go back and check your answers.

3. Try to answer every problem. If you are not sure of the correct answer, make the best guess that you can. Your score on the test will be based on the number of correct answers that you give.

4. Do not put any marks in this test book. You must put *all* your answers on the separate answer sheet you have been given. To mark an answer, find the number of the problem on the answer sheet and put an x in the space over the letter A, B, C, or D — whichever goes with the answer you have chosen.

5. Mark only *one answer* for each problem. If you change your mind about an answer after you have marked it on the answer sheet, completely erase your first answer and then mark your new answer.

6. Be sure that you have printed your name and the other information that is asked for at the top of the answer sheet.

DO NOT TURN THE PAGE UNTIL YOU ARE TOLD TO DO SO

Section Three
VOCABULARY

Directions: This section of the test is designed to measure your knowledge of the meanings of some English words. It is in two parts, and there are special directions for each part. Altogether, there are 75 problems in this section, and you will be given 35 minutes to do them. *Do not stop at the end of Part I but go right on to Part II.*

Part I

Directions: Each problem in Part I consists of a sentence in which one word is omitted. Four words, marked (A), (B), (C), and (D), are given beneath the sentence. You are to choose the *one* word which best completes the sentence.

Look at Example I.

Example I: A _____ is used to cut with.

   (A) knife
   (B) lamp
   (C) horn
   (D) pen

Since a *knife* is used to cut with (but not a lamp, horn, or pen), you should choose the answer marked (A). If this problem were in the test, you would find the number of the problem on your answer sheet and mark choice (A) as shown below.

Example I: (×)   ( )   ( )   ( )
             A   B   C   D

Now look at Example II.

Example II: It must be getting warmer, for the snow is beginning to _____ .

   (A) strain
   (B) melt
   (C) burst
   (D) shine

The correct answer is (B). When snow begins to *melt*, we know the weather is getting warmer. If this problem were in the test, you would mark choice (B) on your answer sheet as shown below.

Example II: ( )   (×)   ( )   ( )
             A   B   C   D

Now go on to the next page and begin work on the problems for Part I.

1. Only one little boy _____ the accident; everyone else was killed.

    (A) absorbed
    (B) survived
    (C) consumed
    (D) reckoned

2. I don't believe the story was really true; it was just an old _____ .

    (A) legend
    (B) errand
    (C) digest
    (D) charter

3. One must handle those dishes carefully, for they're very _____ .

    (A) gaudy
    (B) fragile
    (C) meager
    (D) lavish

4. We were completely _____ by the heavy rain.

    (A) parched
    (B) merged
    (C) drenched
    (D) wedged

5. In the race Beth was _____ against several excellent runners.

    (A) availing
    (B) competing
    (C) expending
    (D) presiding

6. The sudden, strong light made him _____ his eyes.

    (A) notch
    (B) grate
    (C) blink
    (D) warp

7. The roof was supported by six thick _____ .

    (A) trenches
    (B) fringes
    (C) pillars
    (D) torches

8. We couldn't make the cake because we didn't have some of the main _____ .

    (A) ingredients
    (B) compensations
    (C) utilities
    (D) installments

9. The woman hurt our ears with her _____ laugh.

    (A) wee
    (B) frail
    (C) shrill
    (D) limp

10. He offered the committee several possible plans, but they _____ all of them.

    (A) rebuked
    (B) reproached
    (C) repented
    (D) rejected

11. For a while Alex was very angry about the matter, but now he seems _____ to it.

    (A) authorized
    (B) modified
    (C) reconciled
    (D) qualified

12. The man didn't want to answer our question, and so he pretended to be _____ .

    (A) dainty
    (B) prompt
    (C) hardy
    (D) deaf

13. In the dark John _____ over a rock and fell down.

    (A) lingered
    (B) stumbled
    (C) fretted
    (D) rustled

Go on to the next page.

14. When you pick the roses, be careful of their sharp _____ .

   (A) thorns
   (B) shafts
   (C) claws
   (D) sparks

15. The snow was falling in large soft _____ .

   (A) blots
   (B) spines
   (C) flakes
   (D) coils

16. Mary's dog gave a fierce _____ when the stranger approached.

   (A) chatter
   (B) moan
   (C) wink
   (D) growl

17. There is a beautiful view from the _____ of the hill.

   (A) summit
   (B) mantle
   (C) outlet
   (D) ceiling

18. If you don't dry the knife, it will _____ .

   (A) fry
   (B) rust
   (C) shrink
   (D) tint

19. We didn't like the color of the curtains, and so we _____ them a beautiful dark green.

   (A) soaked
   (B) dyed
   (C) sketched
   (D) pierced

20. Coming to a stream, they took off their shoes and _____ across.

   (A) waded
   (B) tugged
   (C) lurked
   (D) hovered

21. The friendly dog ran up to us _____ his tail.

   (A) shrugging
   (B) padding
   (C) wagging
   (D) clipping

22. He fell down when his legs became _____ in the ropes.

   (A) tangled
   (B) huddled
   (C) ruffled
   (D) meddled

23. We piled the books up into three neat _____ .

   (A) stacks
   (B) seams
   (C) stripes
   (D) specks

24. The angry man _____ the door with all his strength.

   (A) spurned
   (B) slammed
   (C) stubbed
   (D) stunned

25. All his shouting left Jack's voice very _____ .

   (A) brisk
   (B) rash
   (C) gaunt
   (D) hoarse

26. The box was fastened shut with two heavy _____ .

   (A) streaks
   (B) scraps
   (C) sprays
   (D) straps

27. As she worked, Grandmother softly _____ a song she had learned as a child.

   (A) grinned
   (B) hummed
   (C) mused
   (D) clutched

Go on to the next page.

28. William went into the garden to _____ the leaves.

    (A) ply
    (B) hew
    (C) tease
    (D) rake

29. The dog has been _____ on that old bone all afternoon.

    (A) grazing
    (B) vexing
    (C) gnawing
    (D) pecking

30. This needle is too _____ to go through the heavy cloth.

    (A) gruff
    (B) blunt
    (C) wan
    (D) stark

31. Bread is made of _____ .

    (A) dough
    (B) sod
    (C) tar
    (D) slate

32. It required a great deal of water to _____ the fire.

    (A) scorch
    (B) thrash
    (C) quench
    (D) daze

33. He had to _____ all his strength to lift the heavy box.

    (A) expire
    (B) excel
    (C) exalt
    (D) exert

34. The warm fire made us so _____ that we soon fell asleep.

    (A) thrifty
    (B) lusty
    (C) nasty
    (D) drowsy

35. The angry crowd began to _____ rocks through the open windows.

    (A) hurl
    (B) tuck
    (C) perch
    (D) screw

Now read the directions for Part II.

Part II

Directions: Each problem in Part II consists of a short phrase beneath which are four words marked (A), (B), (C), and (D). You are to choose the *one* word whose meaning is most nearly the same as the meaning of the phrase.

Look at Example III.

Example III: far away

     (A) worthy
     (B) pale
     (C) distant
     (D) huge

The word whose meaning is nearest the meaning of *far away* is *distant*. Therefore, if this problem were in the test, you would find the number of the problem on your answer sheet and mark choice (C) as shown below.

Example III: ( ) ( ) (×) ( )
                 A   B   C   D

Now look at Example IV.

Example IV: to show the way

     (A) greet
     (B) guide
     (C) guard
     (D) gaze

To show someone the way is to *guide* him. Therefore, you should choose the answer marked (B). If this problem were in the test, you would mark choice (B) on your answer sheet as shown below.

Example IV: ( ) (×) ( ) ( )
                 A   B   C   D

Now go on to the next page and begin work on the problems for Part II.

36. a hard kind of rock

(A) bronze
(B) granite
(C) cane
(D) plaster

37. a great, sudden fear

(A) gossip
(B) panic
(C) famine
(D) gamble

38. a broken piece of something

(A) trifle
(B) cluster
(C) fragment
(D) fiber

39. a place of safety and protection

(A) zone
(B) refuge
(C) site
(D) prairie

40. a short, light sleep

(A) siege
(B) oath
(C) nap
(D) phase

41. very large

(A) gorgeous
(B) mellow
(C) ingenious
(D) gigantic

42. unable or unwilling to speak

(A) mute
(B) gross
(C) harsh
(D) plump

43. a person who lacks courage

(A) butcher
(B) coward
(C) monster
(D) rebel

44. a light, easy conversation

(A) bliss
(B) pose
(C) chat
(D) plea

45. requiring great energy and effort

(A) austere
(B) ardent
(C) abstract
(D) arduous

46. a border

(A) boundary
(B) hearth
(C) circuit
(D) breadth

47. a sweet smell

(A) remnant
(B) taper
(C) fragrance
(D) morsel

48. to keep someone from going

(A) redeem
(B) perplex
(C) detain
(D) beseech

49. a precious stone

(A) lump
(B) chip
(C) crust
(D) gem

50. a package

(A) banner
(B) fabric
(C) parcel
(D) cargo

51. an enemy

(A) dwarf
(B) foe
(C) tramp
(D) heir

Go on to the next page.

52. a danger

    (A) stature
    (B) access
    (C) torrent
    (D) hazard

53. to move with a smooth, easy motion

    (A) glide
    (B) tour
    (C) haul
    (D) loom

54. a container for water

    (A) stool
    (B) pail
    (C) tract
    (D) cot

55. to hold someone back

    (A) provoke
    (B) cherish
    (C) restrain
    (D) banish

56. a young horse

    (A) colt
    (B) fowl
    (C) spider
    (D) frog

57. the upper part of the leg

    (A) scalp
    (B) jaw
    (C) thigh
    (D) skull

58. the cover of a box

    (A) gap
    (B) lid
    (C) mat
    (D) pad

59. to walk with long steps

    (A) stride
    (B) crouch
    (C) stray
    (D) fling

60. to throw away

    (A) discount
    (B) distract
    (C) discard
    (D) disclose

61. a tool used for digging

    (A) sash
    (B) spool
    (C) slab
    (D) spade

62. a statement of one's beliefs

    (A) creed
    (B) fable
    (C) assent
    (D) lease

63. to attack with great force

    (A) allege
    (B) astound
    (C) abound
    (D) assail

64. a small stone

    (A) pebble
    (B) crumb
    (C) panel
    (D) ore

65. to lift something into the air

    (A) sneak
    (B) hoist
    (C) coax
    (D) dodge

66. to consider carefully

    (A) plunder
    (B) stammer
    (C) blunder
    (D) ponder

67. a long, broad board

    (A) tray
    (B) stall
    (C) wand
    (D) plank

Go on to the next page.

68. great anger

    (A) doom
    (B) mode
    (C) quest
    (D) wrath

69. to hold tightly in one's arms

    (A) grind
    (B) blend
    (C) hug
    (D) punch

70. to push roughly

    (A) shove
    (B) chip
    (C) skip
    (D) brace

71. a short period of calm

    (A) fuss
    (B) lull
    (C) din
    (D) pang

72. very unhappy

    (A) wretched
    (B) barren
    (C) selfish
    (D) hostile

73. without hope

    (A) forlorn
    (B) petty
    (C) complex
    (D) haughty

74. acting without pity

    (A) uncouth
    (B) ruthless
    (C) insolent
    (D) boundless

75. clever about practical matters

    (A) pensive
    (B) hale
    (C) potent
    (D) shrewd

Stop! This is the end of the test.